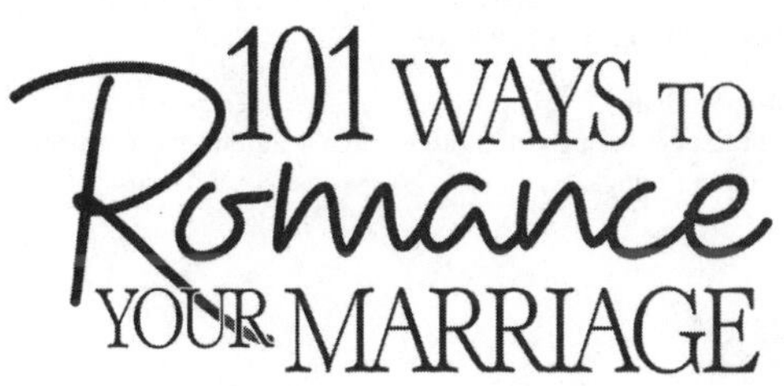

DEBRA WHITE SMITH

EUGENE, OREGON

Cover by Garborg Design Works, Minneapolis, Minnesota

Published in association with the literary agency of Alive Communications, Inc., 7680 Goddard Street, Ste #200, Colorado Springs, CO 80920.

101 WAYS TO ROMANCE YOUR MARRIAGE

Published by Harvest House Publishers
Eugene, Oregon 97402

Library of Congress Cataloging-in-Publication Data

Smith, Debra White.
101 ways to romance your marriage / Debra White Smith.
p. cm.
Includes bibliographical references.
ISBN 0-7369-1125-1 (pbk.)
1. Marriage—Psychological aspects. 2. Love. 3. Sexual excitement. 4. Man-woman relationships—Miscellanea. I. Title: One hundred one ways to romance your marriage. II. Title: One hundred and one ways to romance your marriage. III. Title.
HQ734.S713 2003
248.8'44—dc21 2003001888

Printed in the United States of America

03 04 05 06 07 08 09 / BP-MS / 10 9 8 7 6 5 4 3 2 1

Contents

101 Ways

Love's enemy
has hypnotic power
to drag marital
contentment
into monotony's mire.

Lord,
show me
where I can discover
the surprising,
the spontaneous,
the excitement,
the spark.

I seek
101 ways to
romance my marriage,
unleash desire,
express true love,
revive our fire.

I need
101 ways to
confront monotony,
enrich monogamy,
fulfill passion,
renew vitality.

I long for
101 ways to
a blazing love affair,
a match made in heaven,
a dream come true,
a key to bliss.

Love's Protector,
hear my cry.
Start the fire.
Increase desire.
As I lose myself
to this pivotal hour.

R.N. Hawkins

and

Debra White Smith

PART ONE

Making Your Hero Sizzle

A good man is hard to find.
Once you find him,
do everything in your power to make him happy.

DEBRA WHITE SMITH

1

There is an old saying, "Nothing will do more for a man than the love of a woman." One way a wife loves her husband is to see him as her hero. Allowing her husband to *be* her hero when danger lurks is easy for many women. But husbands need to feel like heroes every day of their lives. I believe that's why they often offer to carry in the groceries or hold open the door or even haul that giant basket of laundry downstairs to the utility room. Although using chivalry to demean women is never appropriate, most men need to feel continually needed—*really needed.* Many of the tasks husbands offer assistance on can be handled by wives; therefore, it's easy for wives to fall into the pattern of saying, "Oh, don't get up. I'll take care of it." In reality, what your husband may really want is for you to gladly accept his assistance and praise him for the "small rescue." Frankly, nothing makes many women more nauseous than an intelligent woman who pretends stupidity with a man. Nevertheless, many men find it exhilarating when a woman can take care of a task alone but welcomes masculine help. At that point, the task goes beyond merely doing a chore and becomes a bonding experience.

Sometimes I wonder if our female ancestors understood the male temperament well when they "accidentally" dropped a handkerchief. The next time you have the chance, try "dropping your own handkerchief" and throw in a saucy wink to nicely round things off.

My Hero

Our newly built home, while not finished, was livable. We decided to move in while we completed the work. I never thought about the various cracks and crevices, as yet unsealed, that allowed free access to all manner of small creeping, crawling, and flying creatures.

And then one night…

Flutter, flutter, flutter…

I open my eyes. In the dim moonlight pouring in through our bedroom windows I see a small, dark object swooping in erratic circles over our bed.

A bat!

Letting out a squeal, I dive under the sheet and give my husband a sharp jab in the ribs with my elbow.

"Wake up!" Jab, jab, jab. "There's a bat in here!"

"Huh? Oh. Whoa!"

There's a sudden thrashing of arms and legs on my left.

"Don't lift the sheet!" I squeak.

My husband's dark, handsome head pokes under my fabric sanctuary. "What?" he asks.

"I said, 'Don't lift the sheet!' And close the bedroom door! I don't want that thing getting into the kids' rooms."

"Right. You stay here, honey. I'll take care of it."

Mindful of my highly agitated state, my strong, ex-Marine carefully slithers out from under the sheet. I pull the covering more closely about me, form a tiny slit for my eyes, and watch.

Clad only in jockey shorts, my hero gets down on his hands and knees and strips the case off his pillow. After whirling it in a circle over his bare head and shoulders, he crawls to the door. He pushes the door shut, then crawls to the closet. In a moment he emerges, on his feet, armed with a tennis racket.

Flutter, flutter, swoop…

The bat heads straight for him. My husband slashes wildly with the tennis racquet. Swish! Swish! Swish!

"You missed! Turn on the light so you can see!" I suggest.

"Can't. He'll take cover."

Flutter, flutter…

Swish! Crack!

I throw off the sheet, eye the gouge in our new four-poster bed, and glare at my husband. "Aim the other way! Don't you dare hit that thing toward—"

Flutter, flutter, swoop…

Swish! Smack!

A small, black object flies past my head and lands on my pillow. I dive back under the sheet to the sound of my husband's maniacal laughter.

"You did that on purpose!" I accuse.

"Never, honey, never," he soothes through a chortle.

I feel a gentle pat, pat on my covered head. The edge of the sheet is tugged from my grasp. "You can come out now, hon. It's dead."

I look at the broken black thing on his tennis racquet and shudder. Giving me a grin that makes my toes tingle, my hero does a cocky swagger to the bathroom to dispose of his vanquished foe.

Splash! Flush…

—Dorothy Clark

To My Dear and Loving husband

If ever two were one then surely we.
If ever man were loved by wife, then thee;
If ever wife were happy in a man,
Compare with me, ye women, if you can.
I prize thy love more than whole mines of gold
Or the riches that the East doth hold.
My love is such that rivers cannot quench,
Nor aught but love from thee give recompense.
Thy love is such I can no way repay,
The heavens reward thee manifold, I pray.
Then while we live, in love let's so persevere
That when we live no more, we may live ever.

ANNE BRADSTREET (1612-1672)

2

Recreate your honeymoon night. Send your husband a special wedding-type invitation announcing that you are taking him on a second honeymoon. If you can't go back to the same place where you stayed, decorate your bedroom in themes from your honeymoon or stay in a similar place. Put on your wedding gown or buy something lacy to wear. Underneath the gown, wear lingerie like what you wore that first night. Find recordings of songs from your wedding and play them in the bedroom or hotel room. On the night of the big event, wait for your husband in the bedroom, and ask him to help you take off your wedding dress.

3

Shop for sexy lingerie as often as you can afford it. You will be surprised at how much anticipation you develop as you think about modeling the new piece for your husband and imagine his response. Most guys accept the fact that their wives aren't model perfect because most ordinary guys aren't perfect themselves. When you realize your body imperfections aren't an issue, you become free to romance your husband with abandon!

4

Roll a single red rose inside your husband's daily newspaper or favorite magazine. Deliver it with a juicy, hot kiss and his favorite beverage.

Watch the sunrise or sunset together.

Amber Miller

On our tenth wedding anniversary, I sent a care package to my husband's job. When he opened it, he found a note that simply said, "Read Song of Solomon 7:11": "Come, my lover, let us go to the countryside, let us spend the night in the villages." I also included a small bottle of massage oil and some scented soap—and the brochure for the cabin I'd rented for the night. He was quite surprised when he put the "puzzle" together, and I felt very sneaky!

—Christie Hagerman

Romance is an attitude, a state of mind. It comes from within. You only have to look for it and develop it. Don't keep wishing you or your husband were more romantic. Do something about it. If you have an image in your mind of what romance is, make the image come to life. Dress the part. Perform the actions. Purchase whatever is necessary. Most importantly, stop preparing to live and start living.

AMBER MILLER

6

Absence really does make the heart grow fonder. My husband works hard every day, and then he comes home to the chaos of a busy household with kids and a dog. Sometimes he feels overwhelmed. When it seems as though we need a little spark, I send him away—to visit relatives, to go skiing, to spend some quiet time in the mountains. At first he loves the peace and quiet, but after about a day and a half, he always comes rushing home, filled with love and usually bearing flowers.

—Mindy Starns Clark

Your Kiss

Your kiss lingers.
Our first kiss went beyond
my lips
into my heart.
There it lingers:
ever sweet,
always moist,
promising,
disturbing,
exciting.

Your kiss captured me.
Your lips created a blaze
of ecstasy
within my being.
There it burns,
ever strong,
always hot,
blazing,
arousing,
fulfilling.

R.N. HAWKINS

7

Call him at work and read a passage from Song of Songs such as 2:8-9 and 2:16-17:

Listen! My Lover!
Look! Here he comes
leaping across the mountains,
bounding over the hills.
My lover is like a gazelle or a young stag.
Look! There he stands behind our wall,
gazing through the lattice....

SONG OF SONGS 2:8-9

My lover is mine and I am his;
he browses among the lilies
Until the day breaks and the shadows flee,
turn, my lover, and be like a gazelle
or like a young stag on the rugged hills.

SONG OF SONGS 2:16-17

8

Find out what your husband's favorite fashion from the past is, such as the 50s, 60s, 70s—or even the 1800s. Declare a night alone at home "A Visit to the Past." Play music from his favorite era. Dress in that style. If possible, prepare a meal from that time. Tell him you're his "date from the past," and let your imagination run wild!

9

Record a personal greeting on a cassette or CD for your husband to play in his vehicle's stereo. Put a sticky note on the disc that reads "Play Me." When your husband plays the recording he will be greeted by you—his lover. You can make the tape as cute and sassy as you like or as sensual as you dare.

What I do,
And what I dream, include thee, as the wine
Must taste of its own grapes.

Elizabeth Barrett Browning

10

I keep all my "romancing" paraphernalia in a bedside drawer. I store candles, matches, scented lotions, and flavored lip glosses. I'm much more apt to use these things and make our time more special if things are conveniently at hand.

—Rosanna Horst

Let him kiss me with the kisses of his mouth—
for your love is more delightful than wine.
Pleasing is the fragrance of your perfumes,
your name is like perfume poured out....
Take me away with you—let us hurry!

Song of Songs 1:2-4

11

Be innovative with simple things. Recently I purchased a mug for my husband. Before I gift wrapped it, I placed sexy underwear along with a note inside the mug. It created an air of anticipation of what was to come. I got a charge out of watching his reaction.

—Cindy Norman

Introductions

Somebody once told me when making introductions to remember this subtle difference. When introducing my husband to others I say, "This is Paul, my husband," rather than "this is my husband, Paul." The first recognizes that Paul is a unique, independent person who chose me to marry. The latter sounds as if his identity is in me. I want to remember that he chose me. It puts a twinkle in my heart.

BRENDA NIXON

12

Fill a big box with tissue paper and place three items inside—a note, your husband's favorite romantic CD, and a small box (a heart-shaped box with a lid is good, but any small box will do). On the note write, "Tonight I've made plans for us. Bring the CD and wear what's in the box." When he opens the box, he'll find it's empty. You take it from there!

—Kathleen Y'Barbo

13

While my husband was growing up, his family always had an Easter egg hunt for all the kids—even when they were old enough to have kids of their own. The first year my husband and I were married, we weren't going to be there for the hunt, so I hid little treasure-hunt notes all around the house with candy or a little gift such as: a picture frame with a picture of us and a clock for his desk. I set the alarm to wake him up early Easter morning. I got up a few minutes before he did and hid in the closet. When the alarm went off, to his surprise there was an Easter basket with a card and a plastic egg with a hint in it to go to the next location. He went along with the scheme. As he moved through the house following clues, I was in the bedroom setting up candles and the final hint. When the second to last hint led him into our room, there were candles lit throughout the room and a giant Hershey's kiss with little kisses in the shape of a heart in the middle of the bed. One more plastic egg note told him to close his eyes and wait. I came out of the bathroom wearing the nightie he liked best. Needless to say, he'll never forget that Easter egg hunt!

—Crystal Olson

14

A few years ago, a dear friend of mine wanted to surprise her husband, who loved Oriental themes. She decided to give him a fun surprise and have him find her at a hotel dressed as a geisha. Another friend and I began working on a kimono. Getting my husband's promise of secrecy, the three of us met at my house during our normal "ladies night out" to measure, cut, and sew for several weeks. Research into the world of the geisha proved to be interesting for all of us. We learned what hairstyles and make-up applications we should use. The day finally arrived. My friend first invited her husband to meet her for lunch at a local Japanese restaurant. After eating, she left the table on the pretext of using the restroom, paid the bill, and slipped an envelope to the waitress asking that it be given to her husband. The message instructed him to head to a local massage therapy place for a prepaid half hour massage. From there she hid envelopes all over town, making a scavenger hunt for him. He had to pick up some chocolates and snacks along with his camera and clothes. The final envelope gave directions to a local bed-and-breakfast. Meanwhile, we women were hard at work. We got to the inn and transformed our brown-haired friend into a dark-coifed geisha, complete with homemade kimono, wig, and makeup. The moment my friend's husband opened the door was priceless. My friend and I dragged him into the room and quickly escaped amid giggles and laughter. We caught a brief glimpse of his stunned face before we closed the door.

This would be easy to do at home as well. Transform your bedroom or any other room in the house for an evening. The cost can be as little or as much as your budget can afford. Sheets could be used to cover the normal furniture. Netting and sheer fabrics are inexpensive as well. Pillows taken from different rooms, some theme music, and a few candles will do wonders for setting a mood. There is no limit to what you can do. I plan to do something similar for my husband using an Arabian Nights theme with me belly dancing for him. Another theme could be a picnic under the stars—made with lights and sheets on the ceiling or under the real stars. It takes a lot of preplanning, but it is worth the effort to surprise your mate with something fun and special neither of you will ever forget.

—Allison Wilson

Christmas Cheer

One year Christmas was hard for my husband because he was ill. To raise his spirits, I created a special Christmas card just for him. It was simple, yet elegant. On the inside, I wrote a love note reiterating bits of our marriage vows: "in sickness, in health, in poor, in wealth" and sharing how I will always be there to listen. This token of our love made that Christmas special because it highlighted our commitment to each other.

MELISSA HOCKING

15

I prepared dinner for the kids ahead of time. After their dinner they became engrossed in a movie. When my husband walked through the door I pulled him into the bedroom and locked the door. I had dinner set for two on a small table. I proceeded to undress him to his boxers and then lovingly massaged his back with oil until he was completely relaxed. Next, I fed him dinner. After dinner, I asked for a massage.

—Beth Goddard

Break the pattern of ordinary in your life. Adventure and romance wait a few feet outside of the circle in which you exist. Step outside and explore the possibilities. You'll never know what you'll discover unless you try.

AMBER MILLER

16

Let your husband know he is one of a kind to you. Like in Song of Songs, let him know he stands apart in your eyes:

Like an apple tree among
the trees of the forest
is my lover among the young men.
I delight to sit in his shade,
and his fruit is sweet to my taste.
(Song of Songs 2:3).

Speak intimately of his body. Describe your husband's hair, eyes, cheeks, lips, arms, legs, and mouth—all his physical attributes:

His head is purest gold;
his hair is wavy
and black as a raven.

His eyes are like doves
by the water streams,
washed in milk,
mounted like jewels.
His cheeks are like beds of spice
yielding perfume.
His lips are like lilies
dripping with myrrh.
His arms are rods of gold
set with chrysolite.
His body is like polished ivory
decorated with sapphires.
His legs are pillars of marble
set on bases of pure gold.
His appearance is like Lebanon,
choice as its cedars.
His mouth is sweetness itself;
he is altogether lovely.
This is my lover, this my friend,
O daughters of Jerusalem.
(Song of Songs 5:11-16)

Let him know you find him attractive.

—Philip Attebery

17

Holiday highlights. If you have a canopy bed, decorate it with pine garlands and Christmas mini lights around the top perimeter. This gives your bed a festive glow. If there is no canopy, secure the lights and pine garlands to the ceiling or upper edge of the walls. Buy a generous supply of pine-scented candles (or scent of your choice). Place them on the dressers and nightstands. Play a Christmas instrumental CD softly in the background. Purchase a special gift you know your husband will enjoy. Shop the lingerie department for a sexy "Mrs. Claus" look. If you like, cut both side seams of a red nightie and apply self-adhesive Velcro strips all the way up and down both sides. You now have a pull-away Mrs. Santa suit.

If you have kids, arrange for them to be away for the evening. You may want to order dinner in so you don't have to worry about the cuisine. If you prefer to cook, arrange a special meal. Light the candles and turn on the music and the twinkle lights. Encourage your husband to prepare for bed in the winter wonderland that was once your bedroom. Sneak into the bathroom, put on your Mrs. Santa lingerie, and have a special gift ready for him when you come out.

—C J and Lynette Sowell

God's Ways Are Always Best

Submit to one another out of reverence for Christ.
EPHESIANS 5:21

The nature of crisis is that when it is yours, it is huge. You can logically measure your problem with someone else's and realize that you do not have it so bad. But that only lasts so long. As soon as your situation hits you in the face you are overwhelmed again.

For months I had been wrestling in my spirit over a crisis of mine.

Due to upheaval in his industry, my husband had been forced to seek employment out-of-state. The problem was that I didn't want to leave New Mexico, and I was beating both of us up over this decision. I was being very unpleasant. Finally I was able to look at my obstacles to this situation. One of my biggest hang-ups was my business. Personally I actually like to move, but my business is established. It has been supporting us during this difficult time. I have great employees, and I love my work. I cannot just up and move.

Once I faced what my fears were, I could stop and ask what would God wanted for my life. It doesn't take a theologian to figure out God's priority. Put my business first, or my marriage first? Hmm...

If I believe in God's Word, which I do, I know I have to put my marriage first. In this case, that meant accepting a move. If God gave me this business, which I believe He did, He would take care of it.

The amazing thing is that the moment I reached this place of decision, my sense of crisis lifted. I was at total peace with the situation. I told my employees, who are all Christians, too, that I would be commuting between New Mexico and Colorado. They applauded my decision.

My husband accepted the position. I got him settled and decorated his temporary home. I cooked him dinners and left him prepared meals in the freezer.

Together we made the best of a difficult situation. For a while, we lived in two states with me, my dog, our main house, and the business in one state and my husband, his job, his dog, and apartment in the next. I made the five-and-half-hour trek between states on the weekends when I wasn't on the road speaking. This commuter marriage lasted six months. We are now back in the same state, and God has blessed my actions! Chuck now has his pick of job opportunities in New Mexico. When I accepted that God's plan was to put my marriage first and submitted to my husband's needs, my personal crisis turned to total peace. After all, I do know God's ways are always best!

MARITA LITTAUER

18

The next time you or your husband has to go out of town, make your husband anticipate his time with you after the separation. Buy a 4 x 6-inch photo album with pockets. (These are often inexpensive and can be found at discount stores.) Cut rectangles out of construction paper to fit inside the pockets of your photo album. Label each one using a black magic marker for each day of the countdown. Slide the paper into the plastic pockets in countdown order. Behind each number, insert a surprise for your loved one. (Use an index card for anything written.) Some ideas are:

- a meaningful verse of Scripture
- a devotional thought
- a picture of the two of you together
- a coupon for the dinner of your mate's choice
- a piece of gum
- a toothpick with the words, "I'd pick you all over again"
- a bookmark
- a coupon for a massage
- a packet of sugar with the words, "You're so sweet"
- a set of movie tickets
- a paper clip with the words, "You hold me together"
- a rubber band with the words, "Bound together by love"

- a paper with your lipstick kiss on it and the words, "I love you"
- a picture colored by a child in the family
- a poem written from your heart
- a card with a magazine subscription
- a packet of hot chocolate with a note that says, "I'm hot for you"

If you're feeling especially creative, decorate the album cover using construction paper, paint, or another medium of your choice. With this countdown, your mate will feel special and loved while you're apart, and he will be eager for your loving arms when you're reunited.

—Christy Barritt

Because I love You

Quirks, flaws, chinks in the armor, those "little things" about our spouse that drive us crazy—when we're dating, "love is blind" ignores these traits. After we get a few years of marriage under our belts, we can see everything. And all those little things—those flies in the ointment—can squelch romantic tendencies. As brothers and sisters in the Lord, we are to prefer and honor one another in love (Romans 12:10). It's easy to be kind and respectful and honor brothers and sisters at church, but how about at home?

I married a neat freak. We jokingly call him Mr. Clean. Of course, my computer desk sticks out in the gleaming kitchen. Papers. Computer discs. Manuscript paper. Jotted notes. File folders. We even joke about my desk, and I know it drives him crazy! I can tell his capable fingers are itching to clear off the piles and toss things and organize.

I think before I change into a cute nightie tonight, I'm going to clean my computer desk, take a digital picture of the wood surface (I know it's under there somewhere), and give my honey a copy of the picture in a card that says, "I love you. Because I do, I honor you in this small way. I'm not perfect, and I'm sure my desk might get cluttered again. But because I love you, I'm trying. With all my heart, Your Boo."

LYNETTE SOWELL

19

Have some glamour shots taken especially for your husband. Many studios offer tasteful yet sexy poses that your husband will find appealing. One of the sexiest shots I've ever seen was of a woman who put on her husband's dress shirt and hat with no slacks. She was well covered, yet the photo spoke of marital intimacy.

20

Most men, and especially my husband, enjoy having their wives make a public display of admiration that appears spontaneous yet tasteful. These three things I've done for my husband went over well.

1. Once when he was away on a business trip and I knew that some of his coworkers would be dropping him off at the house, I hung a bouquet of "welcome home" balloons on the mailbox.
2. One day I stopped by the parking lot of his office when I knew he was in a meeting. I also knew he would be heading to his car afterward with a couple of buddies. I parked next to his car and covered his driver-side window with several small love notes from a Post-It Note pad that I had prepared earlier. I used a simple phrase on each one that I knew

would not embarrass him such as "I Love You" and "You're soooo awesome!"

3. In the bathroom where he gets dressed at work I wrote in bold letters with my lipstick, "I love you, James!" and then pressed my lips to the mirror to make a few kisses. I knew he would like it, but I was even more surprised to see that he didn't erase it; he worked around it to get dressed and left it there all week for all visitors to see.

—K. Jackson

The Phenomenal Freedom to Love

Allow your husband to be a human being, and unconditionally accept and love him—flaws and all. Many women seem to have the idea that husbands are supposed to be one rung below God, and wives are supposed to be one rung below their husbands. Instead of viewing themselves as their husband's spiritual journey-mate and understanding that the husband and wife both complete each other, some women think they are a lesser part of their home and marriage—a tagalong whom God never intended to take spiritual responsibility or to influence their husbands and home. Therefore, these women expect their husbands to be something they cannot be—essentially complete without them or stronger spiritually in all areas than they are.

I have never met one woman who has embraced this erroneous teaching who hasn't become disillusioned with her husband. Many women who believe these falsehoods say something like, "I have one of those kinds of marriages where we are madly in love one day and ready to kill each other the next." Essentially, these erroneous concepts always breed dysfunctional marriages.

Instead of recognizing they embraced erroneous concepts, these wives usually believe their husbands are "defective," and they think other men are not "defective." Over the years the disillusionment grows to mammoth proportions. Disillusioned women don't seduce their husbands.

Understanding that God gave you unique gifts and gave your husband unique gifts, frees you to accept your husband exactly the way he is. Every man will not possess the same set of gifts; neither will every woman. We are individuals created by God, not robots placed in static marriages.

Once you realize these truths, you will stop expecting your husband to manifest his gifts and yours, too. You will fully understand that the two of you are equal halves of a whole. You are indeed a team! And, you will discover a phenomenal freedom to unconditionally love and accept your husband as you see yourself as his seductress, his playmate, his lover, his wife.

21

Does your husband carry a pager? Come up with a number sequence that can say "I love you"—and page him often. My husband and I use the message "1 4 3," which means "I love you" to us. We each feel connected as we think of each other.

—Kathy Collard Miller

You are a garden fountain, locked up,
my sister, my bride;
You are a spring enclosed,
a sealed fountain....
Let my lover come into his garden
and taste its choice fruits.

Song of Songs 4:12,16

22

My husband often enjoys relaxing in a hot bath, especially after a long stressful day at work. So after dinner surprise your husband with a hot bath ready and waiting for him. You can get his attention after he's relaxing by joining him. Or if your husband doesn't like hot baths, you can simply surprise him by stepping into the shower with him.

—Beth Goddard

Romantic Grace

If your husband isn't the most romantic man on the planet, give him some grace. Once you start seriously romancing your husband, it might take a year or two for him to catch on to what you need in your marriage. After I had been romancing my husband for about a year, he looked at me and said, "I don't know if I even know how to be romantic!" Shortly after that, he hired a quartet to serenade me in a restaurant! I believe that a lot of men want to be more romantic than they are. So if there are times when your husband doesn't "get it," an understanding attitude on your part will prove one of the most important concepts in romancing your marriage.

23

Solomon says that his lover is a garden. She responds by inviting him to "come into his garden and taste its choice fruits" (Song of Songs 4:16). Do you ever initiate physical intimacy with your husband? He wants you to! He would love to hear you talk about his body and then lead him into the bliss of physical intimacy!

—Philip Attebery

24

One evening I knew my husband was going to be home late. I lit candles around the bedroom and put on a lacy, white nightie. I arranged the pillows so that I could lie in the middle of the bed and fluffed my lingerie around me. I heard him suck in his breath when he walked into the room. I took his breath away!

—Beth Goddard

How beautiful you are and how pleasing,
O love, with your delights!
Your stature is like that of the palm,
and your breasts like clusters of fruit.
I said, "I will climb the palm tree;
I will take hold of its fruit."
May your breasts be like clusters of the vine,
the fragrance of your breath like apples,
and your mouth like the best wine.

Song of Songs 7:6-9

25

Buy your husband a superhero T-shirt and write him a note telling him why he is your personal hero.

—Cher Anderson

A wife of noble character who can find?
She is worth far more than rubies.
Her husband has full confidence in her
and lacks nothing of value.
She brings him good, not harm
all the days of her life.
She selects wool and flax
and works with eager hands.
She is like the merchant ships,
bringing her food from afar.
She gets up while it is still dark;
she provides food for her family
and portions for her servant girls.
She considers a field and buys it;
out of her earnings she plants a vineyard.
She sets about her work vigorously;
her arms are strong for her tasks.
She sees that her trading is profitable,
and her lamp does not go out at night.
In her hand she holds the distaff
and grasps the spindle with her fingers.
She opens her arms to the poor
and extends her hands to the needy.
When it snows, she has no fear for her household;
for all of them are clothed in scarlet.
She makes coverings for her bed;
she is clothed in fine linen and purple.
Her husband is respected at the city gate,
where he takes his seat among the elders of the land.

She makes linen garments and sells them,
and supplies the merchants with sashes.
She is clothed with strength and dignity;
she can laugh at the days to come.
She speaks with wisdom,
and faithful instruction is on her tongue.
She watches over the affairs of her household
and does not eat the bread of idleness.
Her children arise and call her blessed;
her husband also, and he praises her:
"Many women do noble things,
but you surpass them all."
Charm is deceptive, and beauty is fleeting;
but a woman who fears the LORD *is to be praised.*
Give her the reward she has earned,
and let her works bring her praise at the city gate.

PROVERBS 31:10-31

26

After a particularly amorous evening together, use your husband's bathroom mirror as a messenger of love. Take a red lipstick and write, "Wow!" in big letters on the mirror. He'll get the point and enjoy a sexy chuckle.

Romance turns the kitchen into a fun parlor,
the dining room into a rendezvous,
the bedroom into an island paradise.

R.N. Hawkins

27

I recently asked my husband what his fantasy was. You should have seen the look on his face. His jaw dropped and he asked "Are you serious? Do you really want to know?" I started thinking, *Have I ever asked him what he wants?* The answer was a resounding, "No!" I simply assumed something or tried to figure it out on my own. Asking him that question opened up an entire new level of communication between us. Find a way to sneak the question into your husband's day. Maybe leave a card just for him. Or send him a package at work. Make sure to mark the box "private," and place some sexy lingerie inside with a note: "What is your fantasy? Tell me. I want to fulfill it!"

—Beth Goddard

A Practical Love

During a five-year stretch, neither my husband nor I had time to keep up with minor repairs on our 45-year-old home. During that time frame, we adopted a little girl from Vietnam. That alone was a time-consuming undertaking, yet it was coupled with taking care of our biological son as well. On top of that, I was scrambling to write one book after another, as my writing career exploded; while my husband decided to start his at-home business as well. For a few years we did well to get dinner cooked and the dishes washed, let alone anything extra.

Finally, the day came when my schedule slowed down enough for me to actually see the repairs that needed to be made on our house. My husband is a mechanical genius, but he doesn't consider himself a home-improvement guru. Nevertheless, when I explained to him that I was on the verge of hyperventilating over how bad our house was looking, he immediately rolled up his sleeves and went to work.

After struggling for a whole Saturday to pull up our bathroom tile, he looked at me and said, "Debra, I hate doing this! I hate it! The only reason I'm doing it is because I love you!" The honest frustration on his face mingling with the love in his eyes was as beautiful as any bouquet of roses he's ever offered.

28

The home is an extension of most wives' hearts. Ask your wife to give you a "honey-do" list. If there's any way you can perform the chores, do them for her whether you hate them or not.

29

Most husbands have hobbies like fishing, golfing, or hunting. Sometimes they even use this as a time to get away. But you can take his hobby and create a special time of friendship, bonding, and even romance. One afternoon I took the initiative to suggest that we go fishing. I'm sure my husband was surprised and worried that I would make a mess of everything. You see, when we first began dating he asked if I could bait a hook. This was very important to him. My ready reply was, "Yes, I can do that." Well, we never went fishing after we got married. My reason was, "Well, just because I *can* bait a hook, doesn't meant I *want* to bait a hook." This time I took the initiative to do something he loves with him, and we went to his favorite fishing spot. I took a great interest in everything he said. The day turned out to be a relaxing time for both of us, bringing us even closer. Few things "wow" a man more than a wife who will actually take an interest in and be a part of his hobby.

—Beth Goddard

Attitude Adjustment

My husband doesn't like that I travel. However, traveling has been a part of my life for all my adult years. When I met him, I was teaching seminars all over the country. I think he should be used to it after 16 years of marriage. Instead he likes it less and less.

On the plane on the way home, I often enjoy the relaxing escape of romance novels. As I read, I picture Chuck meeting me at the gate with roses in his hand. Or, at least dropping what he is doing when I walk in the door to kiss and hug me and confirm how much he has missed me. In reality, the plane lands. I deplane and walk alone through the terminal, get my baggage and go to my car. I wait in line to pay for my parking and drive home. Because I like to get home from a trip as soon as possible, I frequently arrive late at night rather than the next day. Chuck is often asleep when I get home. I tiptoe in, drop my bags, and undress in the dark. I crawl into bed beside him and he wiggles his foot against my leg to welcome me home. Hardly the romance novel scene I had painted in my mind.

Recently I flew home the day after the seminar, the day of our sixteenth anniversary. Because it was our anniversary, I really wanted that romance novel scene. The day before I had arranged to have flowers sent to his office with a card that said "Happy Anniversary! Hurry home!" (I had the flowers delivered in the morning in case he forgot what day it was. They would remind him and he'd have time to do whatever he needed to do.) I planned to arrive home before he got off work. I had time to shop for the ingredients to make a lovely dinner. I got home, did the dinner prep work and put it all aside. I went into the bedroom and found something small and black hanging on our four poster bed with an anniversary card. (He hadn't forgotten after all.) I relaxed in a bubble bath and put my present on. I lit candles in the bedroom and put something bubbly in the silver bucket next to the bed with two crystal flutes. It was nearly time for him to get home. I crawled up on the bed and read my romance novel. I waited.

The dogs barked, and I heard his car door. I tucked the romance novel away and placed myself artfully across the bed. I could write a romance novel with the results of my efforts! Because I had sent Chuck flowers, he knew that I had not forgotten what day it was. He knew I'd be waiting and he knew what he had waiting for me. He was excited to see me; glad I had come home. The night left me breathless, and I thought it through in the morning. That was the reaction I'd like every time I get home!

Romans 12:18 tells me that it is my job to do the changing, not to change him. I thought what could I change that would bring about the desired effect? First, I could change my schedule so I came home before he did, instead of after he was asleep. I could fix a special dinner and bring on the bubbly. I could put on one of the many "little somethings" he has given me over the years that

I know he likes and I can place myself across the bed as if in a lingerie catalog. Yes, I could do that.

My next trip I did. It worked again—even without the special day and without the flowers. My next trip I tried it again. It worked again. I had created an attitude adjustment. Although he is still not crazy about my traveling, he loves it when I come home. Without travel, I wouldn't be putting forth the homecoming effort. Maybe travel isn't so bad after all.

MARITA LITTAUER

30

My husband and I are avid outdoors people, and we love to hunt and fish in the fall. In order to prepare for hunting season, we start going to our leased acres several months before deer season begins. During one of these visits to the woods, I secretly packed a picnic lunch. I then set it out in the box stand while my husband put out the corn for the deer. The next time he climbed into the deer stand, he was pleasantly surprised and felt very special. We were able to commune with nature and with each other. He loved it.

—Kimberly Owens

31

Leave a note for your husband when he gets home from work. The note might say something like, "I'm a secret admirer of yours, please meet me at __________ (a special restaurant of your choice) at 7:00 P.M. I'll be the lady in red sitting at the table with a red rose in the vase." Once your husband arrives and finds his "admirer," the two of you can "get to know each other." Maybe, if you hit it off, you can go back to "her place" for dessert. This is fun and definitely gets romantic results.

—Dina Koehly

A Gift of Love

A few weeks before Christmas our vacuum cleaner broke, and my husband told me not to buy a new one because that's what I was getting for Christmas. In a couple of days, sure enough, this big box appeared under the tree—a box just the right size for a vacuum cleaner. Now my husband and I had been married 21 years at that point—way too long for him to still hold onto the belief that household appliances make good gifts. I kept waiting for another gift from him, but it never happened. Christmas morning, as the kids were tearing into their gifts, he handed me the big box. You guessed it—a new vacuum cleaner was inside. Not wanting to ruin Christmas for my four children, ages 5 to

14, I plastered on a smile. After the kids had run off to test out their toys, my husband slid a flat rectangular box out from under the tree skirt and handed it to me with the excuse that it must have accidentally slipped out of sight. My heart soared in anticipation—and then I opened the box to find vacuum cleaner bags. Man, was I mad! The kids were still within earshot so all I could do was thank him through a clenched jaw while I sat there with the dumb vacuum cleaner bags in my lap. He asked me if I'd taken a look at the bags. At this point he was really playing up the finer points of the vacuum cleaner and its bags. I lifted the package and said I really hadn't looked at them.

As I turned the package over, I noticed there was a hole in the plastic wrapper. David told me to open the package and make sure they were all there.

When I did, a little velvet box fell out. Inside was the most amazing diamond ring I've ever seen!

Kathleen Y'Barbo

32

Over the next few weeks, discover the answers to most of these questions. Be prepared to be open and accepting. You'll be surprised what your husband will share if he feels safe and respected.

- What is the most joyful thing that has ever happened to you?
- What has been the hardest experience of your life?
- What are your secret ambitions, your goals for life?
- What are your deepest fears?
- What about me do you appreciate the most?
- What about me would you like to see changed?
- What man or men do you most admire?
- What are your spiritual struggles?
- What do you like best in bed?
- What is your favorite piece of my lingerie?
- What is your favorite color? Favorite restaurant? Favorite dessert?
- What is your favorite song?
- What is your favorite sport?
- Who is your favorite professional athlete?
- What was your favorite class in high school and/or college?
- When you were a child, what did you dream of doing?

- What is your earliest childhood memory?
- What is the one thing you would consider a sexual treat?
- How do you feel about storms? Have you ever been in a tornado? Snowed in?
- What is your favorite brand of underwear?

Softly I Dance with You

Softly, softly I dance with you.
Your strong arms hold me
with a tenderness that makes my heart sigh.
We move together...
without thought...
as one.
Inside my soul whispers,
"How? Tell me why?"

Softly, softly I dance with you
our hearts closely pressed...
touching...
beating...
without words whispering love.
For moments in the crowd we are alone,
and find love renewed.

Too soon, oh too soon, our solitude is over.
The world presses upon us,
forcing us apart.

So whenever I can...
however I may...
softly, softly I'll dance with you,
and only you.

DOROTHY CLARK

33

Cell phones can be a wonderful romance tool. My husband and I both have cell phones that are on the same pricing plan so we have free minutes to each other all the time. My husband has a one-hour drive home from work. Every afternoon when he gets off work I call him and begin our playful game of phone tag. During our many phone calls, I might tell him how much I've missed him, or what we're having for dinner, or even how much I'd like to kiss him. We make wise use of that one-hour drive home and turn it into flirt sessions that start the flames of romance before he gets home.

—Kimberly Owens

The Phone Call

The phone invaded my melancholy.
"Hello,"
the voice whispered in my ear,
softly, sweetly, seductively.
"Darling!"
That simple word set my heart aglow.

Her word reached my heart,
stirred that strange, undefinable feeling
aroused that night when I first saw her,
framed by the late evening sunshine.

Phone calls—wonders of intimacy
for lovers separated by distance.
Whispered words touch ears and lips
uniting lovers in a mystical embrace.

Desire, richer than the physical,
surged agonizingly within my being.
Her words touched my ears with fire,
quelled only later by the moisture of her presence.

Finally, sound gives way to silence.
"Love you,"
echoes in my mind as she says farewell
and space separates lovers again.
"Love you!"
Whispered treasures hoarded in dreams until...

R.N. HAWKINS

34

Rent several of your husband's favorite movies—the ones you normally wouldn't see. Watch them with him while you snuggle and feed him popcorn.

—Beth Goddard

35

Dare to befriend your husband. Get into his space and find out what he loves. Be willing to be his prayer partner and his confidant. Many books on marriage encourage men to find other men to be accountable to. I do not believe this is bad. However, there is an unbelievable spiritual bond that is possible between husband and wife when the two of them agree to get totally clean with God, totally clean with each other, and view each other as intimate friends. My husband and I are growing into a relationship where we view each other as the person we are accountable to. As my husband's confidant, I have agreed to keep all secrets and to not blow up if he confesses an area where he's struggling. He's pledged to do the same. We are pulling together and praying together as friends and lovers. The result on the romance of our marriage is electrifying, to say the least.

36

Try decorating your bedroom from your husband's point of view. My husband and I recently moved into a new home. One day I realized I had always decorated our home to suit my tastes, not my husband's. For example, our bedroom has always been feminine. I decided I should surprise my husband in our new home and decorate the bedroom in a way that would appeal to him. After he went to work one day, not long after we moved in, I rearranged the furniture and decorated the room to resemble a cozy cabin. On the walls I hung several framed outdoorsy prints. I placed his gun cabinet along one of the walls. Above that, I hung an old mirror, and I placed an oil lamp on top of the cabinet. I used an antique chest of drawers that had been in the family for generations and placed an antique mirror above it. I placed my cedar chest at the end of the bed and hung a deer head on the wall. I placed a bamboo runner across the top of our dresser, laid antique books on the runner, and set an oil lamp by the books. I also put a live ficus tree in one corner. For bedside tables, I chose simple round tables and covered them with cream-colored cloths topped with long, antique lace runners. Antique lamps reside on the nightstands. As soon as I can afford it, I'm going to add a faux fireplace. In the bathroom, I used antique mason jars for mouthwash, cotton balls, and toothpaste. I used an old quilt top for a shower curtain, and hung a deer picture on the wall. After decorating the room, I told my husband it was his haven. The bedroom has become our special retreat from the world.

—Kimberly Owens

The Melody Within

A melody beats within,
music seeking words.
Words of love
to sing to you,
passionate, sweet.
A song to tell all...
of love spanning years,
seasoned with laughter,
sometimes tears.
Always sustained
by God's awesome grace
in health, want, or pain.

Oh, if I could only write
that melody of love
that beats within!

A story stirs within.
Pictures crying for words,
words of love
by us to sing
inspired, vivid.
A story to tell all...

of love's long journey,
across rugged times,
uncertainties and sorrows.
God shared all with us.
In Him we place our trust!

Oh, if I could only write
that picture of love
that stirs within.

A passion pulsates within.
Devotion needing words.
Melodies of love
pictured in song
unearthing the story
to be shared with all...
God's unfailing love
centered in His Son,
experienced by lives in concert
under Christ's baton.
Living His symphony,
playing in harmony.

Oh, somehow I will write
that passion of love
that pulsates within.

R.N. Hawkins

37

One evening, I decided to create a romantic atmosphere in the bedroom. While my husband was in the shower, I slipped on a new, slinky, black ooh-la-la, folded the covers down to the foot of the bed, lit a candle, and sprayed perfume on the sheets. As a final touch, I clicked on the bedside radio for some soft background music. Soon, I discovered the radio was set on a gospel station. Before I had time to change it, my husband walked into the bedroom. A deep bass voice from the radio belted out the old gospel song, "How long has it been?"

—Kristy Dykes

38

I keep romance burning in my marriage by occasionally *not* wearing makeup or fixing my hair. Each time I sport the natural look, I nearly have to arm myself with a wooden spoon to ward off my husband, "Mr. Octopus Hands." For years I believed my dear husband found me gorgeous and irresistible in my natural glory. But one time I pushed him away and asked why he seemed to be all hands and fingers when I was at my worst. He stood to his full height, and his lips formed a slow smile. "I don't have to worry about messing you up," he said. "You already are."

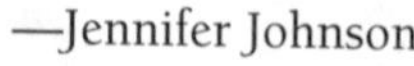

—Jennifer Johnson

39

Boast about yourself to your man. Your husband will enjoy hearing you speak sensually of yourself. Tease him with why he should be romantically interested in you. Solomon's lover speaks of her beauty, chastity, breasts, and his contentment with her. She is aware of her imperfections and that others are prettier, but that doesn't stop her from having confidence in the romance she offers him. The idea of monogamy creates romantic excitement. It excites your spouse to remember that you saved your body for him and that now it is all his! Remind your spouse of your permanent devotion to him and watch the romance ignite!

—Philip Attebery

40

When you are mad at your husband, go into the kitchen and bake his favorite dessert. Acting out love enables you to more easily forgive. And it will blow your husband away!

—Chris Sanders

And the LORD God caused a deep sleep
to fall upon Adam and he slept:
and he took one of his ribs, and closed up the
flesh instead thereof; and the rib, which the LORD God had
taken from man, made he a woman,
and brought her unto the man.
And Adam said, "This is now bone of my bones,
and flesh of my flesh: she shall be called Woman,
because she was taken out of Man." Therefore
shall a man leave his father and his mother,
and shall cleave unto his wife: and they shall be one flesh.
And they were both naked, the man and his wife,
and were not ashamed.

GENESIS 2:21-24 KJV

On our tenth anniversary I surprised my husband by renting the honeymoon suite at a local hotel. I had the staff put candles and chilled fruit juice with wine glasses in the bathroom for us. Then, I took my husband there after we dined out. While he carried in the overnight case, I hurried into the bathroom, ran a tub of bubbles, climbed in, and then called him. Unknown to me, he had turned on the TV and was watching football.

I called him again. He came into the bathroom and blankly looked at me waiting there surrounded by bubbles and candlelight. His mind obviously on football, he asked, "What?"

For a second, I decided the romance was dead. But I was determined not to lose the moment. So instead of getting angry, I propped one bare heel on the edge of the tub, held up my glass of juice, and asked with innuendo, "What do you think?"

At that point, his eyebrows rose and he said, "I'll be right back." He disappeared for a moment to turn off the TV, and then he joined me.

I tease him about it now, and he says, "But, honey, it was the Broncos!"

—Kim Sawyer

What does love mean?

A group of professionals posed the question, "What does love mean?" to a group of 4- to 8-year-olds. The answers they got were broader and deeper than anyone could have imagined.

"When my grandmother got arthritis, she couldn't bend over and paint her toenails anymore. So my grandfather does it for her all the time, even when his hands got arthritis, too. That's love."

Rebecca—age 8

"When someone loves you, the way they say your name is different. You know that your name is safe in their mouth."

Billy—age 4

"Love is when a girl puts on perfume and a boy puts on shaving cologne, and they go out and smell each other."

Karl—age 5

"Love is when you go out to eat and give somebody most of your French fries without making them give you any of theirs."

Chrissy—age 6

"Love is what makes you smile when you're tired."

Terri—age 4

"Love is when my mommy makes coffee for my daddy, and she takes a sip before giving it to him to make sure the taste is okay."

Danny—age 7

"Love is what's in the room with you at Christmas if you stop opening presents and listen."

Bobby—age 5

"If you want to learn to love better, you should start with a friend whom you hate."

Nikka—age 6

"There are two kinds of love. Our love. God's love. But God makes both kinds of them."

Jenny—age 4

"Love is when you tell a guy you like his shirt, then he wears it every day."

Noelle—age 7

"Love is like a little old woman and a little old man who are still friends even after they know each other so well."

Tommy—age 6

"Love is when mommy gives daddy the best piece of chicken."

Elaine—age 5

"Love is when mommy sees daddy smelly and sweaty and still says he is handsomer than Robert Redford."

Chris—age 8

"When you love somebody, your eyelashes go up and down and little stars come out of you."

Karen—age 7

"You really shouldn't say 'I love you' unless you mean it. But if you mean it, you should say it a lot. People forget."

Jessica—age 8

PART TWO

Making Your Lady Swoon

A woman wants a man she can look up to who won't look down on her.

STAN TOLER

42

I wanted to surprise my husband with a gift certificate to a local golf course and tell him he was meeting a friend there at a certain time. However, I deliberated which friend I should invite. Finally, after a lot of thinking, I decided to tell him about my plan and ask him what friend he wanted to invite. He thought for a few seconds and then smiled. "I want *you* to go with me," he said. I glowed with pleasure because I never imagined he'd choose me. So I went golfing with him. We spent several hours together on the golf course and had a blast! This was one of the best gifts my husband has ever given me. I felt so honored and adored to know that he'd choose me over all his male friends.

43

Jack pushed himself off the flimsy raft to drown in the icy North Atlantic so Rose could survive. That scene grabbed the hearts of girls and women to make *Titanic* an all-time box-office blockbuster. *Titanic* caught my attention when I read how a Michigan wife and mother had viewed the three-hour, ten-minute film 23 times—and she planned to go back to see it again. *What's up with this lady?* I pondered. Because I was writing a series of books for girls, I had to know:

I polled girls in school classrooms over several weeks. An eighth-grader of 14 had seen *Titanic* in the theater more than a dozen times before her mother bought the video. "Now I watch it every day after school with my 18-year-old sister," she giggled. *Aberration?* I queried more than a dozen classes in schools where I worked as a substitute teacher. Most 10- to 18-year-old girls had viewed *Titanic* at least twice—many three, four, even six times. One thing stood out: Without exception the girls' favorite scene was when Jack drowned so Rose could live. Later, I took this concept to a group of about 100 ladies—mostly wives in their 40s and 50s who were members of the Athens, Texas, Literary Club. I told them of my experiment with schoolgirls regarding *Titanic*. This group of ladies was in agreement with the younger generation. Godly women really do want a husband who will die for them....

They want a husband not just willing to die, but really to die to all self interest and put her first. Sound drastic, guys? Yet God put into the heart of every female—whether prepubescent or adult—the longing for a man who will die for her. Jesus pointed out that only in death to the self—made possible by His own death—can our lives be fruitful and "produce many seeds" (John 12:24). This is especially important to men who wish to have satisfying relationships with their wives.

You can't understand why your lovely wife is so hard to get along with? You'll never reach her until you pull a Jack-with-Rose trick. Just die, guy.

—Eric Wiggin,
"Dead Men Make the Best Husbands."

Within the heart of every woman
lies the desire to be
loved by a man who will
surrender his life for her.

ERIC WIGGIN

44

Ask your wife to tell you what her most hated household chore is, and then promise to faithfully perform that chore for one year. After that year, ask her if she'd like you to add another chore to your list or switch the first chore with another one. Then commit to another year of serving her in this fashion. Annually evaluate your commitment.

45

I value my wife's contribution to our family. I hug her often and encourage her in her writing and speaking ministry. When I recognize that her spirits are low, I try to lift her up. The way I think about it, romance sometimes involves the intangible such as verbal encouragement, listening, and reaching that inner person only I see.

—Paul Nixon

46

Regularly take the time to be still and listen to your wife. Look into her eyes, stroke her face, hold her hand, ask nothing in return. Simply let her know that every word she says is of monumental importance to you. Commit 30 minutes a day to simply listening to your wife and valuing her enough to focus solely upon her. Even if what she wants to talk about really doesn't concern you, she will feel like a treasured queen and her adoration for you will increase.

47

Arrange to take a day off and declare it a special holiday for your wife. If you have kids, make arrangements for their care. If your wife has a career, secretly arrange with her boss for her to take the day off. That morning, tell her you're her "knight in shining armor," awaiting her beck and call. Then do whatever she wants the whole day. Depending on your wife's interests and tastes, a list of suggestions might include: shopping, checking into a hotel with a Jacuzzi and spending the day lazing around, going to garage sales, painting her toenails, swimming, hiking, or golfing. Whatever you plan, make certain it's something *she* genuinely enjoys.

48

At your next anniversary, buy a flower for every *month* you've been married, rather than every year. If you've been married more than a year or two, this bouquet will be *huge*. That's the whole point! To keep this economical, scout out discount department stores that sell fresh flowers. You can buy whole bouquets of 20 to 30 mixed flowers for a few dollars.

49

My husband made a certificate on the computer that said, "This love certificate entitles Sophie to a full body massage at the time of her choosing. This coupon is valid for one year. Be sure to ask about our 1,000 kisses promotion."

—Sophie Laurie

Love is patient, love is kind.
It does not envy, it does not boast,
it is not proud. It is not rude,
it is not self-seeking,
it is not easily angered,
it keeps no record of wrongs.
Love does not delight in evil but
rejoices with the truth.
It always protects, always trusts,
always hopes,
always perseveres. Love never fails....
When I was a child, I talked like a child,
I thought like a child,
I reasoned like a child.
When I became a man,

I put childish ways behind me....
And now these three remain:
faith, hope and love.
But the greatest of these is love.

1 CORINTHIANS 13:4-8,11,13

50

Write a love note to your wife "just because." List all the reasons you think she's beautiful. Include several traits from her personality, her spirituality, and her physical attributes.

Knight in Shining Armor

Strong, gentle, caring, loving you.
You are my knight in shining armor,
though sometimes the shine is hard to see
when daily hassles cloud the view.
But you're always there—
steady, quiet, and sure.
What would I do without you—
my anchor, my playmate, my lover.
How empty my life would be
without strong, gentle, caring, loving you!

DEBRA WHITE SMITH

51

My husband jogs almost every day. When he returns, he always has a miniature bouquet of wildflowers in his hand. He finds these growing in an open field by our house and picks one or two. Sometimes they're just weeds that have bloomed, but they're still quite intricate and beautiful. After picking them, he jogs the rest of the way home, carrying the flowers in his hand. When he walks through the door, he hands them to me. "They're from God's garden," he says. I place them by my computer keyboard and enjoy them the rest of the day.

—Martha Bolton

The Joy of Our Bond

Spring opened its heart in verdant grandeur.
The sun rose, majestic, ruling the eastern sky.
I looked to the west to see the morning star,
hanging in the still-gray heaven like a
jewel on a virgin's breast.
Come beloved, bring your light and warmth,
to my waiting arms and throbbing heart.
These eyes behold your strength and honor;
my fingers caress your ivory skin.
Do you seek me for your wife,
great lion with velvet paws?

The dowry I bring you is filled
only with love, worship, and honor.
Summer came and my love showed me,
from a hill high above the valley,
all the land his sheep would graze,
and the brook that watered his pasture.
He took me to the bridal chamber in his father's house.
Close by his side I lay,
and told him of every passion I felt.
He pledged eternal love and steadfast care.
Each day we walked the fields of grain
and out to the shore of the sea.
No shadow ever crossed our path,
nor pain, nor want brought our souls worry.
The golden winds of autumn turned our bower
to a place of quiet charm.
My belly grew ripe with child;
his father's arms held us both.
Pain and labor brought great reward.
The child in my arms was a son,
a lion cub for his father's pride,
molded in the regal image of a king.
My breasts gave milk for his body;
each day he grew like a mighty cedar.
With wonder I watched his manhood approach,
knowing someday I would have to give him to another.
Winter's gray seemed to come so swiftly;
our fields were brown and barren.
Laughing children called from beyond the hill.
The brook ran ever so slowly; life was ebbing away.

My love came near me,
and with arms even then so strong and true,
held me close to his faithful heart,
whispering words of comfort and hope.
His kisses still enraptured me,
and his embrace brought waves of desire.
Never will cold or want or age,
diminish the joy of our bond.

Robert Osborne

52

Wanting to see the display of meteors that would be in the sky for a few nights, my husband drove us out to the country, where there were no city lights and nothing but black, inky night full of twinkling lights and meteors streaking across the sky. As we sat on the hood of the car and watched the magical scene, I kept thinking, *Now this is romantic*.

—Wanda Brunstetter

53

After dinner give your wife the evening off. Insist on doing the dishes. And after the kitchen is clean, spoil her with a lavish foot massage and ask nothing in return. If you really want to astound her, repeat this for one week.

We Love Because...

We love because
God first loved us!
He claimed our lives
with the great love of Calvary.
From that awesome reality
comes a love eternally.

We love because
God first loved us!
He brought us together
to live under His Word
embraced with a passion
to know and serve the Lord.

We love because
God first loved us!
He linked our hearts in love
allowing us to show
abiding, growing devotion
regardless of life's flow.

We love because
God first loved us!
He called us to Himself
gave each to the other
His pleasure to treasure
His grace beyond measure.

That is why we love because
He first loved us.

R.N. Hawkins

54

Invite your wife on a date with a theme of her favorite color. For instance, if her favorite color is red, call her and tell her you are going to take her on a "Red Date" that night. Do your best to incorporate the color red throughout the date. The following are a host of suggestions. Use these ideas or create your own ideas for your special date.

- Ask her to wear her favorite color.
- Wear a tie or suit or shirt in that color.
- Make reservations at a restaurant and request a tablecloth in her favorite color.
- Take her on a picnic and use a cloth in her favorite color.

- At the beginning of the date, present her with a bouquet of flowers in that color.
- Arrange to eat as much food as you can from that color group.
- Buy your wife a piece of jewelry with a stone in her favorite color. Depending on your budget, you can spend a few dollars or hundreds on the jewelry. Jewelers and department stores now offer a wide array of colored cubic zirconiums set in sterling silver that are quite affordable.
- If jewelry isn't your wife's interest, buy her a new T-shirt, or hiking shorts, or whatever she most enjoys, in her color.
- At the evening's close give her a gift bag full of several new pieces of lingerie in her special color. Who knows! She just might treat you to a style show!

Security comes when I'm in love with
somebody who loves me back.

Shelley Winters

55

While I battled traffic all the way home during my daily commute, my man and my two kids were conspiring to wow me speechless! They gathered a couple of my favorite books, including one I'd been reading. Then the kids made a fruit tray, garnished with cheese and crackers. My husband found some votive candles and scattered them around the bathroom. He drew a hot bath for me and arranged the tray with the books and snacks on the closed commode lid. The kids picked some roses from the bush outside, and scattered the petals from the living room door, down the hallway and into the bathroom. A special invitation was taped to the front door, with instructions for me to relax and enjoy!

When I pulled into the driveway, it felt like any other day. Exhausted, I prepared myself for the typical barrage of questions and my family needing me. But when I saw the note and opened the front door to silence, I started to wonder. I followed the rose petal trail, calling out to my family. No answer. I heard our *Sounds of the Ocean* CD playing from the direction of the bathroom. Still no family. Just the occasional crying of seagulls.

I opened the bathroom door to see lit candles, a steaming bath, fluffy towels, my robe, a wonderful snack, and iced tea in a crystal goblet. Then I heard giggles from behind our bedroom door. I gave them all hugs and kisses, then disappeared for an hour in my private spa.

What a super concept, getting the family involved. My son learned about making things special for a hard-working lady, and my daughter learned what she should expect from her husband one day. Not only did my kids enjoy surprising mom, but my honey held a relaxed and ready-for-lovin' wife in his arms that night!

—Lynette Sowell

I am a hopeless romantic,
and my wife can attest to the hopeless part!

Stan Toler

56

On New Year's Eve or July 4th, buy a special round of fireworks just for your wife. Before setting them off, tell her she's about to get an example of how she affects you. Then light the fireworks and watch her eyes sparkle.

57

For our last wedding anniversary, my husband surprised me with a trip to Boston and New York. He sent me a cute email card in which he told me that we would be taking a trip and the dates we would be going—one word on one line at a time. At the bottom of his message he included websites for me to discover each place we were to visit, each hotel, and the Broadway plays. I felt like a kid in a candy store!

—DiAnn Mills

Time Out

Two bored children,
inquisitive minds,
carefree escapades,
household havoc.
My biblical meditation assaulted.
My concentration distracted.
My spirituality fractured.
My carnal nature stirred.

I rose up,
captured my "space invaders."
We rumbled, raced around a park,
swings...sodas...

We walked back home,
hand in hand.
I worshiped God today
as the four of us played.

Wife under pressure,
frazzled beyond measure.
I'm weary and stressed.
Mutual consternation.
Emotional frustration.
Dangerous combination.

We rose up,
canceled weekend business,
left the house mess.
Picnic on the beach.
Lips within reach.
Love refreshed,
heart in heart.

We worshiped God today
as the three of us played.

R.N. AND MARY HAWKINS

58

Because I get up earlier in the mornings than my husband to work out, he always makes the bed, brews the coffee, and has the newspaper ready for us to read together.

—DiAnn Mills

59

Solomon calls his lover a "lily among thorns" (Song of Songs 2:2). He speaks intimately of her and describes her cheeks, neck, eyes, temples, hair, teeth, lips, mouth, breasts, feet, thighs, waist, nose, head, figure, and breath. He also compliments her attire and perfume. What lady would not be encouraged by a husband's flattery of her entire anatomy and her taste in what she wears? A wife can be primed toward romance by consistent and ongoing verbal admiration from her husband!

—Philip Attebery

Sometimes in our earnestness to do life right,
we forget to play!
When was the last time you and your love played?
If you can't remember, well…it's playtime!

Dolley Carlson
Mr. and Mrs. Gifts from the Heart

60

On my birthday, even though I knew we would probably do something that evening, I felt a big letdown when my husband left for work and the kids went to school. Was I ever surprised when soon after the children departed, Richard showed up at the back door. As a special birthday present, he'd taken the day off work. We went shopping, out to lunch, and had several romantic hours alone.

—Wanda Brunstetter

61

My husband loves to give me surprises. It doesn't have to be a special occasion for him to suddenly announce, "You have one hour to pack for a ____-day trip. These are the kind of clothes you will need." He always has the smallest detail worked out.

—DiAnn Mills

62

I cut out 30 small white strips of paper and wrote on each of them romantic things I would do for my wife. I put them into a pill bottle. I taped my own prescription on the outside of the bottle and gave directions for her to take out a piece of paper each day. Some of the items were "honey dos" and others involved dinner out at her favorite dining place or something as simple as a free back rub. What a month of fun!

—Stan Toler

63

For Valentine's Day last year, I sent my wife a dozen roses and went shopping at Victoria's Secret for her. I purchased sleepwear as well as some of her favorite lotions and had them gift wrapped. I packed her luggage and picked her up at work. I then drove her to the nicest Marriott in our town. We stayed Friday and Saturday night.

—Stan Toler

But since there is so much immorality,
each man should have his own wife,
and each woman her own husband.
The husband should fulfill his marital duty to his wife,
and likewise the wife to her husband.
The wife's body does not belong to her alone
but also to her husband. In the same way,
the husband's body does not belong to him alone
but also to his wife. Do not deprive each other except
by mutual consent and for a time, so that you may
devote yourselves to prayer. Then come together again
so that Satan will not tempt you because
of your lack of self-control.

1 Corinthians 7:2-5

64

Take a couple of weeks to discreetly learn what your wife's favorite breakfast includes. After she's asleep one Friday night, sneak out to an all-night grocery store and buy every item on her list. Surprise her the next morning with breakfast in bed.

Love Letter

This morning
the mailman delivered a kiss
in an envelope.
A letter from my husband.
His heart hidden beneath a stamp.

The kiss to my heart was sweet.
It lingered long—
moistened eyes,
aroused joy.

This morning
the mailman delivered a dream
in an envelope.
A letter from my lover.
His love hidden beneath a stamp.

The dream to my mind was real.
It aroused memories,

created intimacy,
overruled misery.

This morning
the mailman delivered a hug
in an envelope.
A letter from my other half.
His thoughts hidden beneath a stamp.

The hug to my body was warm.
It vanished time,
chased tension,
calmed fears.

This morning
the opened door revealed my husband.
No envelope.
No stamp.
Just my handsome man,
with a kiss,
a hug—
a dream come true.

R.N. Hawkins

65

What unique ways can express your excitement for your wife and the pleasures of romance in your marriage? How can you illustrate to her that she is your choice out of all the women in the world? Solomon used creative and sensual illustrations to describe his romantic feelings toward his lover. He says that even if 60 queens, 80 concubines, and a countless number of virgins were available to him, she would be his choice for a bride:

Sixty queens there may be,
and eighty concubines,
and virgins beyond numbers;
but my dove, my perfect one, is unique,
the only daughter of her mother,
the favorite of the one who bore her.
The maidens saw her and called her blessed;
the queens and concubines praised her.

SONG OF SONGS 6:8-9

Solomon gets steamy by describing his lover's breasts as clusters of fruit in a palm tree. He says, "I will climb the palm tree, I will take hold of its fruit!"

—Philip Attebery

A Yellow Rose

Our yellow rose tradition began one bleak and dreary winter long ago. In October 1980, I bid farewell to my mother after her bitter battle with liver cancer. One month later, my heart, heavy with grief, nearly broke when my 38-year-old husband suffered a severe heart attack. For two weeks, I traveled to his bedside with a single yellow rose. It had to be a yellow rose—"The Yellow Rose of Texas." Not an easy task when we were 3,000 miles from Texas in the dead of winter in New England. But, after all, like the song lyrics tell, he was the only rose for me. On the first anniversary of his heart attack, my husband was in Texas at a new job. I sent a yellow rose south, and he sent one north in remembrance. The next anniversary, I was teaching a reading lesson to my fifth grade in Houston, Texas, when the school secretary walked into my classroom with a bouquet of two yellow roses. "Is it your birthday or wedding anniversary?" she asked. Imagine her surprise when I replied, "Neither. It's the second anniversary of my husband's heart attack." That dreary day 22 years ago could have been a tragic memory; instead, we mark it as a reminder of our constant love. Some wives may long for diamonds or jewelry. Others for chocolate or candlelight dinners. For me, a single yellow rose on the anniversary of my true love's heart attack is the only thing for me.

JUDYTHE HIXSON

66

At a speaking engagement where I was the keynote speaker and particularly nervous, my husband sent flowers 30 minutes before my talk. It eased my nerves and his sweet words on the card made me love him even more.

—DiAnn Mills

67

Needing to get away by ourselves, but too poor to stay at a hotel, my husband gathered up our old tent, sleeping bags, and camping gear, and off we went to the woods. What could be more romantic than sitting around the campfire, roasting marshmallow, and listening to my husband play his harmonica and sing?

—Wanda Brunstetter

Love Letters and Notes

"I guess I could write forever about your wonderful self and what you mean to me...I love you, I want you, and I need you! I also thank the Lord for you and what He's done in our lives!" This quote is from a letter I wrote to my wife on our two-month wedding anniversary. Occasionally my wife and I read some of those old love letters composed during our courtship. They remind us of why we thought getting married to each other was a good idea, and they often spark some of the premarital excitement we had some dozen years ago. You may find it hard to remember when your spouse had such a romantic vocabulary, but have the courage to read your old love letters again anyway. Approach the letters with some humor and be sensitive to the possibility that your reactions to his or her letters could embarrass your spouse. If you know the letters contain a lot of "mushy stuff," use that to your advantage. Let your spouse know before you read the letters that you intend to charge up the romance and follow through on all the "hugs and kisses" written therein!

You might also enjoy reading letters you received at or after your wedding: "I know that you will always be happy together"; "you are getting a really wonderful guy"; "she's fantastic." Read the sentiments or listen to the words recorded at your reception: "I wish that your love for each other will always be so strong that it can only be surpassed by the love you will feel when you see Jesus in heaven!"

"Because of your love for the Lord, you can have something so few people in this world have. The love you have for each other can grow each year. Think of what it can be 50 to 75 years from now! Be faithful in serving the Lord."

These are just a few comments written by members of our wedding party. My mother had pencils and heart-shaped note paper available at our rehearsal dinner and invited everyone to write us notes of encouragement. It was a great idea. She collected the notes in a small "wishing well" and gave them to us before we left that night. My bride decided to pack the notes for our trip, and we read them during our honeymoon. Occasionally, we both read some of those old notes of encouragement. They remind us of why people who are truly significant to us thought our getting married was a good idea too. It reminds us of our terrific wedding day, and this can start the romantic juices flowing.

Do you have something that reminds you of what friends and family have said or done to encourage your marriage? You may have specific wedding gifts, videos, cards, photographs, or e-mails that remind you of why others believed your marriage was a good idea. If you are planning a wedding, consider how you might create such opportunities for those close to you.

PHILIP ATTEBERY

My best birthday present is never something wrapped *in* paper; it's always something *on* paper—the nonglossy side of 8 to 12 feet of butcher paper, to be exact. Who wouldn't melt to come through her front door and find a handmade banner singing her praises plastered across one whole wall of the dining room? The words are always so nice that I don't mind getting another year older. My birthday banners feature colorful, two-foot-high letters proclaiming such gems as:

27 and Made in Heaven

29 and She's Real Fine!

31 and Shines Like the Sun

33 and Full of Glee

34 with Looks Galore

35 and Queen of the Hive

36 and You're My Pick

38 and Lookin' Great!

40 and Lookin' Sporty

41 and Full of Fun

42 and Still Brand-New

44 and Ready for More

45 and Lookin' Alive

50 and She's Real Nifty

60 and Cute as a Pixie

My husband started the birthday banner tradition the year we were married. Then, when the kids came along, he involved them in the fun too. They start dreaming up the slogan weeks in advance. On the day before or the day of my birthday, they find an excuse to get me out of the house while they go to work.

The banner symbolizes much more than fleeting sentiments captured on paper. Any purchased birthday card can provide that much. The slogans on my banners may seem campy on the surface, but they show me my worth in their eyes by the creative energy and time out of their busy lives to give me a personalized thrill on my special day.

Anyone can afford to give such a thrill to his spouse. And it doesn't have to be limited to a birthday. The idea is truly all-purpose. An anniversary. A holiday. An olive branch after a fight. Or no particular occasion. Cost is minimal—creativity unlimited. Combine the banner with the more traditional wooing of flowers or a candlelight dinner, and you've created a lifelong memory. And I'll bet your spouse won't let you throw away that length of butcher paper!

On the other hand, for the flamboyant and well-heeled, hiring a skywriter or renting a billboard would be another adaptation of the concept. For me, though, the simple, private tradition between my husband and me oils our romantic clock quite nicely. Another year. Another banner. Another tender seal upon our union.

The following suggestions are for anniversaries:

1 and You're My Hon

2 and We Still Coo

5 and Our Love Thrives
6 and We Still Click
7 and We're in Heaven
10 and I'd Marry You Again
15 and Still My Queen
20 and I Love You Plenty
29 and Our Hearts Entwine
30 and Still My Flirty
33 and Made for Me
38 and Our Love Is Great
40 Years and My Heart Still Cheers
41 and We've Just Begun
44 and the Best Is in Store

Banners are expressions of delight that proclaim their message for all to see.

—Jill Elizabeth Nelson

You Are Beautiful, My Love

You are beautiful, my Love.
You have a beauty the years cannot take away...
a beauty enhanced by the
laughter lines around your eyes,
the tinges of gray in your hair.

The source of your beauty is not found in cosmetics.
Your beauty comes from within.
Your spirit rejoices in God's grace
and seeps to the surface.
Joy, shining through sparkling eyes,
flashing smile, caring fingers.

You are beautiful, my Love.
You have become more beautiful as youthful glow
is overtaken by senior radiance.
Your body may not fit into yesteryear-size dresses,
but it still has the power to captivate me.

I thank God for the wonder that in your body
was formed, carried, and delivered
our wonderful children.
God in His grace has made your body
not only for my pleasure
and the source of our family,
but also the temple of His Holy Spirit.
His indwelling Presence creates the
fragrance of Heaven within you...

the perfume of Christ.
His perfume touches others through your
attitude and unconditional acceptance.

You are beautiful my love.
I thank God continually for you.
I thank Him for His mercy in allowing me to
drink of your beauty all these years.
What a joy it is to know that I will behold
your redeemed beauty,
in His presence, eternally.
Praise His wonderful name!

R.N. Hawkins

69

Be willing to pray with your wife. Many wives long for their husbands to share prayer and Bible reading with them. As my husband and I grow in this joint endeavor, I am amazed at how this spiritual pursuit bonds us as nothing else. It's very encouraging for me to hear my husband pray for me; he likewise finds peace and comfort in my praying for him. When we ask God's blessing upon our union, we carry with us an inner sense that the force who created us is anointing our endeavors. Whether your marriage is on the rocks or thriving, committing to regularly praying together will add a power and strength to your marriage you never imagined could exist.

70

My husband and I have been married almost 35 years, and I must confess that he is the romantic. Since the first years of our marriage he has made a habit of leaving me the letters ILY ("I Love You") in different places around the house and in various mediums. The first one I can remember was made out of huge strips of toilet paper on our kitchen floor. He has also spelled it out on the kitchen table with candy and toothpicks. One time he tore the letters out of pieces of paper and put them in a letter and mailed them to me. We often leave little notes for each other on the kitchen table or front door and sign them ILY.

—Rose Allen McCauley

You have ravished my heart,
my sister, my spouse;
you have ravished my heart
with one look of your eyes,
with one link of your necklace.
How fair is your love,
my sister, my spouse!
How much better than wine is your love,
and the scent of your perfumes
than all spices!
Your lips, O my spouse,
drip as the honeycomb;
honey and milk are under your tongue;
and the fragrance of your garments
is like the fragrance of Lebanon.

SONG OF SOLOMON 4:9-11, NKJV

71

Instead of buying your wife cut roses, buy her a rose bush. Plant it near the front door. Every time the bush produces a crop of fresh blooms, cut your wife a new bouquet. The bush will soon become a special symbol of your love. (Do be aware that rose bushes require regular care. For this to work, you need to consult with a plant expert about proper, long-term care.) *Never* let the care of the bush shift to your wife. Instead, tell her that this is a labor of love from you to her. Every time she sees you fertilizing the rose bush or spraying it for insects, she'll be impressed with your thoughtfulness and love.

When you choose your rose bush, consider the meanings of each of these rose colors and choose according to what suits your wife and your relationship.

Red: Love, beauty, courage, and respect

White: Purity and innocence, silence or secrecy, also reverence and humility

Pink: Appreciation, "Thank you", grace, perfect happiness, and admiration

Dark Pink: Appreciation, gratitude

Light Pink: Admiration, sympathy

Orange: Desire and enthusiasm

Red and White: Given together, these signify unity

Red Rosebud: A symbol of purity and loveliness

White Rosebud: Symbolic of girlhood

Thornless Rose: Signifies "Love at first sight"

72

Many women are like fine automobiles that need to sit and purr awhile before driving. Any good mechanic knows you get the best performance out of a vehicle if you treat it with tender loving care and baby it some. The same holds true for women and sex. Mark one day a week as "Project Seduction." Start that morning with a phone call from work, telling your wife you think she's the most spectacular woman alive. An hour or so later, perhaps, e-mail her with a compliment about how nice she looks in her new dress. Mid-morning, call and ask her to meet you for lunch. During lunch whisper in her ear how she turns you on. From there, drop a few subtle innuendoes. Mid-afternoon take time to call her and offer a few details of how you are planning to make love to her.

You can also take this concept on a trip. If you and your wife are driving somewhere for any length of time, don't waste the time with idle chitchat. Instead, begin the whole process with a few sincere compliments that grow into talking seductively to your wife. If you invest some time into talking sexy to your wife, you'll be surprised at how "revved" her engines will become.

We love him, because he first loved us.

1 John 4:19 KJV

Stars

Yes. I love the stars. I love them.
I love the way they shine
for the Hand that created them.
I love their jewel-like magic,
diamonds that dreams are made of.
I love their unfathomable number,
forever on fire to always inspire.

Yes. I love the stars. I love them.
Come with me. Come with me. We'll fly to the stars.
We'll embrace them and soak up their splendor.
We'll embrace them and blaze with His love.

Yes. I love the stars. I love them.
We are stars. We are stars.
We are the carriers of light.
The light of the universe.
We twinkle forth a message
the world longs to hear.

He loves you. He loves all.
Come with me. Come with me.
Embrace this Giver of Light.
His flame of love will transform dark night.
Yes. I love the stars. I love them.

Debra White Smith

To Rome with Love

Love

So, the year's done with!
(Love me for ever!)
All March begun with,
April's endeavour;
May-wreaths that bound me
June needs must sever;
Now snows fall round me,
Quenching June's fever—
(Love me forever!)

ROBERT BROWNING

73

Insist on taking your wife golfing or fishing or hunting or whatever your hobby involves. Arrange for a bouquet of flowers or special gift to be placed at a strategic place—for instance, in your tackle box or your golf bag. Then, ask her for something from the exact spot where you've placed the gift so she'll find it and be surprised.

74

A few years ago on the snow-covered hillside outside our kitchen window my husband stamped out a big, 50-foot heart with the letters C+R in the middle. I didn't notice it when I looked out the window, so he suggested we take a walk (another romantic thing to do, especially if holding hands). I still didn't notice the heart the first time we walked past it. A neighbor stopped and asked us if we had noticed someone making tracks in our field. He said he tried to read the message and thought it was someone's initials. That's when I finally realized what my husband had stamped out! The love letter in soil was even more noticeable a couple days later when the snow began to melt. Then the green grass showed where he had stamped and the white heart and letters outlined in green were very visible to me and everyone else who drove by.

The next year I thought I would top him, and I stuck press-on glow-in-the-dark stars on our bedroom ceiling in the shape of a heart with ILY (I love you) in the center. But he was not to be outdone! That year he took a bucket of red paint and climbed up on one of our barn roofs and painted a big red heart with C+R in it. It's still there and so is the heart of stars on our bedroom ceiling. Whoever said "love is for the young" didn't know my husband—my very own knight in shining armor still, after 35 years!

—Rose Allen McCauley

75

I chase after dreams like a child chases after summer butterflies. My husband knows this and chooses presents accordingly. For example, early in my marriage I had a passion for volleyball. I joined three different leagues. I ran my own jump training sessions and lifted weights regularly. Despite the fact that I spent many evenings away from him playing volleyball, my husband bought me an expensive leather volleyball to show that he understood and supported my love for the sport. The ball was a nod of acceptance that said, "You are free to chase the butterfly."

He seemed amused when I became intent on cartooning. I checked out a variety of how-to books from the library, but soon discovered there's more to being a cartoonist than doodling. Seeing my flustered determination, my husband bought me an art kit, paintbrushes, and paper. His gift lifted my spirit. It seemed to say, "That butterfly you're chasing after looks pretty lofty. Nevertheless, here's a butterfly net to help you reach higher." I didn't become a cartoonist, but I did design a school mascot and win first place in an amateur art contest.

When I decided I wanted to learn Spanish, my husband uttered not one word of discouragement. He loaned me his old Spanish books from high school. He corrected my horrid pronunciations with a patient smile until I progressed far enough to be able to converse in slow, awkward sentences. I glowed like a schoolgirl whenever I heard my husband tell his friends I taught myself Spanish. His words encouraged me, as if to say, "Just the act of pursuing butterflies is a worthwhile endeavor."

Finally, after 15 years of marriage, I discovered something that makes my heart sing: writing. I realized writing always hovered near my soul, a beautiful butterfly waiting patiently since childhood for me to notice its flight. After I won my first writing contest, I joined a writer's group. My husband gave up some of his evening commitments so I could attend the meetings. His sacrifice let me know I was free to chase the butterfly. After my first publication, my husband handed me a butterfly net in the form of a notebook and fancy pen. As I continued to learn and grow in the craft, he shared my joy. His encouraging words let me know that whether or not I succeeded, my efforts were worthwhile.

And so I possess an unlikely ensemble of gifts that I treasure most: a ball, paintbrushes, a smile, and pens. By these things, my husband has taught me what it means to romance our marriage. I learned the actions, attitudes, and words with which you gift your spouse demonstrate that you believe in him or her. I learned that when your mate chases butterflies in the sun, it is your privilege to be the gentle wind whispering, "Your dreams are important. Follow your heart. I'm right behind you."

—Lori Z. Scott

76

Imagine your wife is the lover you always dreamed of having in your life. If she *were* that lover, how would you treat her? You would *ask her* what she dreams of in a lover, and do everything in your power to live that. Life is too short to not take advantage of every opportunity! Don't become so obsessed with your work, your bills, your car, your home, that you neglect the most important relationship in your life—the one with your wife. Cultivate the relationship. Pursue your wife as you did before you were married. Before you know it, your wife will become your dream lover.

—Amber Miller

The voice of my beloved!
Behold, he comes
leaping upon the mountains,
skipping upon the hills.
My beloved is like a gazelle or a young stag.
Behold, he stands behind our wall;
he is looking through the windows,
gazing through the lattice.
My beloved spoke, and said to me:
"Rise up, my love, my fair one,
and come away.

For lo, the winter is past,
the rain is over and gone.
The flowers appear on the earth;
the time of singing has come,
and the voice of the turtledove
is heard in our land.
The fig tree puts forth her green figs,
and the vines with the tender grapes
give a good smell.
Rise up, my love, my fair one,
and come away!
"O my dove, in the clefts of the rock,
in the secret places of the cliff,
let me see your face,
let me hear your voice;
for your voice is sweet,
and your face is lovely."

SONG OF SOLOMON 2:8-15 NKJV

77

My husband turned our loft into a beautiful garden, complete with plants from all over the house, soft lights, music, and chilled juice. There, we had our own romantic picnic—all without leaving the house.

—Rebecca Barlow Jordan

PART THREE

The Hero and the Lady

There are three things that are too amazing for me, four that I do not understand: the way of an eagle in the sky, the way of a snake on a rock, the way of a ship on the high seas, and the way of a man with a maiden.

PROVERBS 30:18-19

78

With three teenagers in the home, wise to every move we made, it was hard for my husband and me to find any time to talk together. It seemed every sentence was interrupted or commented upon by the kids, even if what we were talking about had nothing to do with them. Even an innocent kiss on the cheek received whistles, jeers, or "I know what you two are going to be doing!" Short of triple homicide, we devised a clever plan for privacy. After dinner we took our coffee cups and wandered out to the car, rolled up all the windows and locked the doors. We warned the children not to come out unless somebody was seriously injured. Those few moments alone in the car, sipping coffee and talking about whatever we wanted, were like dewdrops on a thirsty tongue.

—Linda Rondeau

79

Kick your way through fallen leaves. Gather them into a pile and jump or fall into them together.

—Amber Miller

One Flesh

You hold me so close,
my chin pressed to your chest.
Is that your heart's rhythm
or mine?
One Flesh.

Your smile immediately, spontaneously
leaps onto my face.
I can't even fight it
when I'm angry with you.
One Flesh.

Sad news assaults.
Your tears well up.
Yet they fall from my eyes.
Your pain.
My pain.
Our pain.
One Flesh.

Sitting in church,
worshiping together.
One.
A melodious instrument.
A joyful noise.
You softly kiss my forehead during prayer.
One Flesh.

Dancing together
in shoeless feet to soundless music.
A celebration of nothing,
but of everything we are.
A kitchen dance
for no special reason...
just because.
One Flesh.

Together forever,
no thoughts of escape
from this lovers' bond.
So grateful God picked me
to become part of "us."
One Flesh.

Cheryl Norwood

80

Reluctant at first, my husband finally agreed to join me for an early morning pedicure at my favorite nail salon. The soon-as-the-doors-opened appointment ensured the privacy I perceived his ego needed. He was so amazed at how rejuvenated his feet and legs felt he suggested we go for a walk along the nature trail in a nearby state park. Already in warm-ups and tennis shoes, we stopped for bottled water and a trail-mix snack. Later, we shared this "lunch" atop the most beautiful peak in the park. Walking for his diabetes and our health now includes an occasional pedicure and a special getaway for just the two of us.

—Lin Harris

Free yourself. Change your pattern.
Jolt the old, familiar things into new,
unfamiliar things. Be the first to make the effort
to change, and your spouse is sure to follow.

Amber Miller

81

We made a commitment years ago to keep one weeknight open. That is our date night. If it is not an emergency, we don't let anything interfere with our special night. We do different things such as go out for coffee or a movie, or we just have a quiet evening at home with romantic music, candlelight, and conversation.

—Susan Neufeld

82

Last June I went on one of my husband's business trips with him. We drove to Denver, stopped for dinner in Loveland, Colorado, on our way in, and then we went to the Wal-Mart Supercenter. We looked at our watches and gave ourselves 30 minutes to each go our separate ways in the store and buy some things to make the evenings special. We had so much fun! We bumped into each other a couple of times and both of us quickly tried to hide what we were going to purchase. As the next two days unfolded we set times to break out the items we had bought. It really was a lot of fun.

—Kim Maskell

83

If you've been married awhile, buy an "oldies" CD that features popular love songs from when you were dating. Spend an evening listening and swaying to the music. As you share memories from those years when you were first falling in love, you'll be surprised at how new your love will feel.

84

For many years, we have followed the advice of pastor/evangelist Paul Burleson, who says to "Divert Daily," "Withdraw Weekly," and "Abandon Annually." My husband and I find ourselves more and more loving to "Abandon Quarterly" to a nice hotel or wonderful bed-and-breakfast. We've made lots of fantastic memories, and it keeps our marriage fresh with anticipation and romantic enjoyment. We started doing this when our children were small—and I am now a grandmother.

—Rebecca Barlow Jordan

Marriage should be the beginning of a richer,
deeper romance based on shared moments,
shared memories, shared family...on listening,
flirting, paying attention to each other's feelings
as well as each other's words.
Don't behave like a "boring wife,"
behave like a seductress.
Don't behave like a "tired husband,"
behave like a forbidden lover.

Amber Miller

85

My wife and I have a lot of fun shopping for clothes with what I call "romantic intentions." It involves finding a place for our kids to stay a night or two and reserving a hotel room out-of-town. We check in to the hotel and immediately look for a place to shop. (We don't have to leave town, but being away from home creates a little more freedom for shopping with romantic intentions.) The purpose of the trip is not so much to buy something we need as it is to enjoy seeing each other in nice or romantically stimulating attire.

"Romantic Intentions" will help your romance, too. First, set the ground rules. Let your spouse have the say in what he or she would like to see you "try on" at the store. Remove the usual limits of particular styles, colors, or price and have some fun! Let your spouse see you in things you would not normally wear. It might spark some romance and passion to just look at you. Maybe he imagines or wants to see you in nice evening wear or a short skirt. Maybe she wants to see you in jeans a size smaller than you normally wear. Enjoy looking at each other until you can't stand it—and remember to get the full benefit of the price you're paying for that hotel room.

Consider planning a financial budget for your romantic shopping spree. It should include the expenses of having someone take care of your children, the hotel, travel, meals, and a determined amount you can spend on the purchase of clothes. Remember that you don't have to travel far to do this. Just plan to spend time in a city comfortable to you. You may also need to prepare your spouse before you leave. I suggest giving each other an idea of the type of clothes you may be asking the other to try on. This might be done by showing pictures from a clothing catalog or by pointing out items in a store where you regularly shop. Look forward to the idea and have the courage to enjoy shopping with "romantic intentions!"

—Philip Attebery

Seduction

The act was deliberate,
slow...focused....
Reaching across
barriers...distances.

The move was secretive,
enticing...stimulating.
It was well-rehearsed
yet spontaneous,
seducing...capturing.

The desire was whispering,
waiting...longing...
linking lovers intimately
with...
a wink!

R.N. Hawkins
and Debra White Smith

86

My marriage has *benefited* from an online affair. My husband frequently has job assignments that keep him away for months at a time, with only weekend visits home. During those periods when he is away, we have an online affair *with each other* to keep romance alive. We flirt online and look forward to the weekends he is home.

—Candy Arrington

87

My husband and I exchange heart-gifts and cards. Once a year we like to get creative and artistic with these home cards. On the inside we write three things we really appreciate about our mate. These are usually character qualities our partner has shown over the past year or areas of growth we have noticed. Then we each give one gift from our heart. It is usually a promise to do something special for our partner during the next year. It can be something like praying daily for him or her, beginning a weekly date night, focusing on appreciation of the spouse, or helping with a particular need. Heart gifts have helped keep the romance alive in our marriage.

—Carrie Turansky

88

Create an inexpensive adventure date. Go to the train station or bus station and catch the first ride to wherever it's going. Explore the area together and learn something new. No matter where it is, you'll be seeing it together. You'll find something there for just the two of you, and it will make the journey special.

—Amber Miller

89

Sharing your partner's dreams and goals really helps you connect on a heart level. Why not plan a special night out and prepare several questions that relate to goals and dreams. Ask your mate, "What would you like to do as a job or ministry if money were not an issue?" or "What do you see yourself doing in five years?" or "What vacation would you take if you could go anywhere in the world?" These are fun questions that will give you insights into your mate's dreams and desires. Then consider how you can encourage your partner to reach some of those goals.

—Carrie Turansky

90

My husband was in the air force for four years and was sent to Thailand twice during that time. One of the ways we romanced each other during those times was writing letters almost every day. Something else we did every day was read our Bible and pray at the same time, allowing for the 12-hour time difference. Before he left I copied a list of New Testament readings, and we both read through the whole New Testament the first year he was away, reading the same selection at the same time. Even though we were separated physically by 12,000 miles, we were joined spiritually. A revival speaker once gave an illustration I have never forgotten. He said marriage is like a triangle with God at the apex and each spouse at the two points of the base. As we each grow closer to God, the base moves upward and we grow closer to one another.

—Rose Allen McCauley

91

My wife and I have a standing lunch date once a week. It doesn't matter what day of the week or which restaurant we choose, as long as we get away by ourselves. Sometimes we have a picnic in the city park or drive to a hilltop lookout for a scenic getaway.

—Ronnie Johnson

92

Combine romance with a little housework. During the day take a couple of hours to clean your car, collecting all the spare change you find under the seats and between the cracks. Do the same inside your house with the couches and chairs. Clean them and collect the loose change. Combine all the change you find, along with the money in your wallets and pockets, and make an evening out of it. It might only be enough to split an ice-cream sundae at a local fast-food restaurant. Or, you might be surprised and find enough for some fine dining and even a rented movie afterward! Be creative with your use of the buried treasure you've uncovered.

—Christy Barritt

If you have any encouragement
from being united with Christ,
if any comfort from his love,
if any fellowship with the Spirit,
if any tenderness and compassion,
then make my joy complete
by being like-minded, having the same love,
being one in spirit and purpose.
Do nothing out of selfish ambition or vain conceit,
but in humility consider others better than yourselves. Each of you should look not only to your own interests, but also to the interests of others.

PHILIPPIANS 2:1-4

93

I try to leave unexpected gifts on my wife's desk at work when she is elsewhere. She really loves it when I surprise her with flowers. A gift on her birthday and our anniversary is expected, so I choose to celebrate this way on days when she doesn't expect it. Every time someone comments on the flowers, it reminds her that I want everyone to know we are in love.

—Ronnie Johnson

94

Carve out some couple time, even if the getaway doesn't seem like a date. My husband and I are members of a county Political Executive Committee; we know one evening every month we will be working together as a couple for causes and issues we believe in and support. My husband was on the committee first and recruited me. One of the reasons I joined was because it gave me the opportunity to work with my husband. This togetherness has strengthened our marriage because it refocuses us as a team.

—Janet Kawash

Rabbi Ben Ezra

Grow old along with me!
The best is yet to be,
the last of life, for which the first was made:
our times are in His hand
who saith "A whole I planned,
youth shows but half; trust God: see all nor be afraid!"

Robert Browning

95

Poetry has been a major part of the romantic journey my husband and I share, especially the poetry of Elizabeth and Robert Browning. When we renewed our vows at a marriage retreat, poetry fueled our romance. Sharing verses from the Brownings' love poems boosted our resolve. We framed our silhouettes, done at Montmartre Art Colony in Paris, as a reminder of our commitment. In the center, in calligraphy, are the words of Elizabeth Barrett Browning's "Sonnets from the Portuguese": "How do I love thee? Let me count the ways...." When we lost our parents and our own mortality sank in, Robert Browning's "Grow old along with me, the best is yet to be" became our mantra. We share the whispered words frequently during hugs. One Christmas I tracked down an antique, leather-bound copy of the works of Robert and Elizabeth Browning for my husband. While clearing the remains of the gift-opening chaos, I looked up to see him rub his hand softly across the cover. His face glowed with true appreciation, which made me love him more. We view love poems as a traditional standby we often neglect that can help keep that spark of romance fresh.

—Judythe Hixson

Love in a Life

I.

Room after room,
I hunt the house through
we inhabit together.
Heart, fear nothing, for, heart, thou shalt find her—
next time, herself!—not the trouble behind her
left in the curtain, the couch's perfume!
As she brushed it, the cornice-wreath blossomed anew:
yon looking-glass gleamed at the wave of her feather.

II.

Yet the day wears,
and door succeeds door;
I try the fresh fortune—
range the wide house from the wing to the centre.
Still the same chance! She goes out as I enter.
Spend my whole day in the quest,—who cares?
But 'tis twilight, you see,—with such suites to explore,
such closets to search, such alcoves to importune!

ROBERT BROWNING

Life in a Love

Escape me?
Never—
Beloved!
While I am I, and you are you,
so long as the world contains us both,
me the loving and you the loth,
while the one eludes me, must the other pursue.
my life is a fault at last, I fear—
it seems too much like a fate, indeed!
Though I do my best I shall scarce succeed.
But what if I fail of my purpose here?

It is but to keep the nerves at strain,
to dry one's eyes and laugh at a fall,
and, baffled, get up and begin again—
so the chase takes up one's life, that's all.
While, look but once from your farthest bound
at me so deep in the dust and dark,
no sooner the old hope goes to ground
than a new one, straight to the self-same mark,
I shape me—
ever
removed!

ROBERT BROWNING

96

Let everyone know you love someone! My wife's desk is next to the check-out counter in the front of a library, and she displays candid snapshots of me in sight of students checking out books. When a new student sees a picture of me showing off a large bass or posing on vacation, he often figures out my wife and I are married. It makes me feel good to know she wants everyone to know we are together.

—Ronnie Johnson

97

One time we went to the hospital to call on a woman in our church. We had just stepped onto the elevator. Nobody else was in there with us, and Richard pulled me into his arms, gazed lovingly into my eyes, and said, "Have I told you lately how much I love and appreciate you?"

—Wanda Brunstetter

How Do I Love Thee

How do I love thee? Let me count the ways.
I love thee to the depth and breadth and height
my soul can reach, when feeling out of sight
for the ends of Being and ideal Grace.
I love thee to the level of every day's
most quiet need, by sun and candle-light.
I love thee freely, as men strive for right;
I love thee purely, as they turn from praise.
I love thee with the passion put to use
in my old griefs, and with my childhood's faith.
I love thee with a love I seemed to lose
with my lost saints—I love thee with the breath,
smiles, tears, of all my life!—and, if God choose,
I shall but love thee better after death.

Elizabeth Barrett Browning

98

Visions of hearts glowing with precious memories float from my romantic remembrance box. During our 39 years together, and through our combined efforts, we have kept our romantic love alive. My memory box testifies to that. As I examine each heart in my mind's eye, a smile curves my lips. Some memories make me blush: My seductive whisper promising an evening straight from Song of Solomon inadvertently broadcast via my husband's speaker phone to an office filled with top-level executives. The e-mail about his sexy fragrance lingering in our room that received the "hot pepper" warning flag for explicit content as it went through the company server's filter.

Then there are the memories of special events and special places. Bed-and-breakfast weekends, vacation getaways, hand-in-hand walks through places far and near: Butchart Garden in Victoria, Canada, a field of heather in Scotland, the streets of New York City, around our block, around the mall. Simple touches or smiles that link us....Unusual memories, traditional memories that have made life's journey with my mate sweet and our love stronger.

—Judythe Hixson

The Unspoken

I was...
attracted by your walk,
arrested by your grace,
accepted by your look,
aroused by your touch.
The pleasure of the unspoken.

I was...
beguiled by a smile,
bewitched by a wink,
bothered by a frown,
broken by a tear.
The power of the unspoken.

I was...
charmed by your style,
captivated by your sparkle,
comforted by your spirit,
consumed by your love.
The wonder of the unspoken.

R.N. Hawkins

99

Since my husband and I can't afford to go out to dinner, pay for a babysitter and the like, our alone time comes in very simple ways. Every Sunday when the kids go outside to play or are otherwise occupied, my husband and I sit down together and do the Sunday crossword. Ever since we started dating, the Sunday crossword has been a ritual that we *always* do together. And our vocabulary has increased twofold.

—Tracy Farnsworth

Don't rely on prepackaged romance to solve your problems. Relish the everyday things that can add romance... a walk on any beach, hand-in-hand, at midnight. Enjoy the gifts of life that are free. Don't spend all your time striving for what's not free, and then make yourself too exhausted to enjoy it.

Amber Miller

100

One year, my husband and I had very little money to celebrate our anniversary, so I dropped off our two children at my parents' place, came home, fixed us a candlelight dinner, and then got dressed in my prettiest dress. After dinner, my husband and I built a fire in the fireplace, hauled our mattress off the bed, and slept in front of the glowing embers. It was one of the most memorable anniversaries we've ever had.

—Wanda Brunstetter

Many waters cannot quench love;
rivers cannot wash it away.
If one were to give
all the wealth of his house for love,
it would be utterly scorned.

SONG OF SONGS 8:7

101

After the kids go to bed and the house gets quiet, I run a bubble bath in our garden tub and light several candles. My husband and I turn off the lights, sit in the tub in the candlelight, and enjoy the silence and each other. It is a very relaxing and romantic way to end our day.

—Kim Davis

Love's Seasons

When we met my heart knew there was a Springtime.
Love had come to my heart.
We were young.
Our lives created a melody of color,
love's rhapsody.
You softened my brashness,
I freed your shyness
and God's grace perfumed our togetherness.
It was Springtime.
It was love.

When we married there was the joy of Summertime.
Love had found commitment.
We were young
our lives tasted the heat of passion
love's nourishment.

We discovered each other
admiring, caring
and God's grace enriched our togetherness.
It was Summertime.
It was love.

When our children grew, left, it was Autumntime.
Love had proven itself.
We were mature.
Our lives colored by life's grandeur,
love's testimony
that this season of marriage
has unfading glory
and God's grace transforms our togetherness.
It was Autumntime.
It was love.

When retirement came we knew it was Wintertime.
Love has lingered long.
We are seniors.
Our lives crowned with hope's warmth
love's privileges
with its special dignity
filled with memories of joy
and God's grace filling our togetherness.
It is Wintertime.
It is Love!

R.N. HAWKINS